FLY!

A BRIEF HISTORY OF FLIGHT ILLUSTRATED

BARRY MOSER

FLY!

A BRIEF HISTORY OF FLIGHT ILLUSTRATED

WILLA PERLMAN BOOKS
AN IMPRINT OF HARPERCOLLINS PUBLISHERS

Fly!
A Brief History of Flight Illustrated
Copyright © 1993 by Barry Moser
Printed in the U.S.A. All rights reserved.

Library of Congress Cataloging-in-Publication Data
Moser, Barry.
  Fly! : a brief history of flight illustrated / Barry Moser.
    p.   cm.
  "Willa Perlman books."
  Includes bibliographical references (p.)
  Summary: Highlights sixteen episodes in the development of
aviation ranging from balloons to the space shuttle. Also includes
a time line and historical notes.
  ISBN 0-06-022893-8. — ISBN 0-06-022894-6 (lib. bdg.)
  1. Flight—History—Juvenile literature.   [1. Flight—History.]
I. Title.
TL515.M69   1993   92-30960
629.13'09—dc20   CIP
                                                                  AC

1   2   3   4   5   6   7   8   9   10

❖

First Edition

◁ Title page illustration: Otto Lilienthal flying one of his monowing gliders.

The text display type for FLY! *A Brief History of Flight Illustrated* was composed
in Bell, Tekton, and Tekton Bold. The paintings were executed in transparent
watercolor on paper handmade for the Royal Watercolor Society by
Simon Green of the Barcham Green Mills, Maidstone, Kent, Great Britain.
The transparencies were made by Gamma One Conversions, New York, New York.
The color separations were made by Fine Arts Repro House Co. Ltd., Hong Kong.
The entire book was printed by Worzalla Publishing, Stevens Point, Wisconsin, on
Patina Matte made by Lindenmeyr Book Publishing Papers, New York, New York.
Bound by Worzalla Publishing, Stevens Point, Wisconsin.
Production supervision by Lucille Schneider and John Vitale
Designed by Barry Moser and Christine Kettner

For Clyde Edgerton
DUSTY'S AIR TAXI AND BUSH PILOT SERVICE
*and all the generations of writers who
were also flyers*

—B.M.

INTRODUCTION

WHEN I was a boy, I had two dreams: to be an artist and to be an aviator. I became an artist because I could draw well and because I stuck with it. But because I lacked good eyesight, I never became an aviator. Not a *real* aviator, anyway. As a little guy, I pretended I was an aviator when I drew airplanes on the big sheets of brown wrapping paper my daddy brought home from work. I sometimes even wore a leather aviator's cap and goggles when I drew these airplanes, putting my imaginary ships into breathtaking dives, effortless rolls, and dizzying spins. And, of course, since World War II was just over, I flew countless combat missions and unleashed all sorts of mayhem on my family's enemies. It seems to me now that most of my childhood drawings were of airplanes—along with monsters, animals, trees, and human faces and figures. These are still my favorite subjects, and I use them as often as I can in illustrating my books. Unfortunately, I rarely get the opportunity to make pictures of airplanes anymore. So here is a book that is the result of the memories of those childhood flights of fancy, of my continuing interest in aviation, and of an excuse to make pictures of airplanes again.

FLY! *A Brief History of Flight Illustrated* did not start out as a history; it just turned out that way—a short, chronological, episodic history of men and women and their flying machines. It begins not with the origins of flight (which date back thousands of years, to the Chinese kite and the Australian Aborigines' boomerang), but with the invention of the hot-air balloon and the transportation of animals and humans into the ether. Each illustration is accompanied by a brief text that tells of a particular historic event or period, with a more complete historic context of that event being given in the Historical Notes at the end of the book. At the foot of each page is a time line that tells the reader what else was going on in the world in science, politics, sports, the arts, etc., at about the same time as the event depicted.

It should be noted that the illustrations are, in most cases, accurate depictions of machines and events. However, machines built and events taking place prior to the invention of photography (and thus having no photographic documentation) are subject to the artist's interpretation, invention, and whimsy.

I would like to thank Rebecca Davis for all her sweet kindnesses; Ray Wagner of the San Diego Aerospace Museum; and the staff of the National Air and Space Museum, Washington, D.C., especially Bob Dreesen, Dan Hagedorn, Larry Wilson, and Tim Cronen, for their invaluable help.

—Barry Moser
Bear Run, Hatfield, Massachusetts, 1992

1783, American Revolution ends • 1784, first school for the blind founded • 1784, Benjamin Franklin

THE FIRST ASCENT

KITES, rockets, and boomerangs had been around for a long time before 1783, when Joseph and Étienne Montgolfier loaded a duck, a sheep, and a rooster into a basket and sent them flying suspended beneath a hot-air balloon. These three animals have the distinction of being aviation's first aeronauts.

The Montgolfiers sent the animals up to make sure that the air above was breathable. Once they knew that it was, they sent a man aloft in the same balloon. That man's name was Jean François Pilâtre de Rozier, the first human aeronaut.

◁ The Montgolfiers' balloon at Versailles, France.

invents bifocals • 1786, commercial manufacture of ice cream begins • 1789, French Revolution begins

1838, Samuel Morse demonstrates the telegraph • 1842, first use of a general anesthetic • 1849,

THE FIRST FLIGHT

SIR George Cayley, an Englishman, was responsible for the very first human flight. It was 1849 when Cayley, who is known as "The Father of Aerial Navigation," tucked a ten-year-old boy into a three-winged glider and pushed him down a hill. After bouncing and bobbing and jolting for a bit, the whole contraption lifted off the ground, and the boy became the first human being to fly in a heavier-than-air flying machine.

◁ Cayley's "boy glider" at Scarborough, England.

Elizabeth Blackwell becomes the first woman doctor • 1851, Herman Melville's *Moby-Dick* published

1861, American Civil War begins • 1865, Abraham Lincoln assassinated • 1868, African-American men

OTTO LILIENTHAL

IN 1891 Otto Lilienthal built his first practical glider and was the first man to truly achieve sustained and controlled flight. He did this over two thousand times in simple, lightweight gliders. He learned to fly by *flying*—controlling his flight by shifting his weight. By flying so often, Lilienthal accumulated vast experience of the various influences that weight, wind, and air exerted on his gliders during flight. He kept meticulous notes on these flights and phenomena, and those observations, combined with the widely distributed photographs of him flying, exerted powerful influence on all subsequent pioneers in flight.

◁ Lilienthal gliding at Lichterfeld, Germany.

gain the right to vote • 1876, Alexander Graham Bell invents the telephone • 1895, X rays discovered

1896, first motion picture shows in New York City • 1898, Marie and Pierre Curie discover radium

THE WRIGHT BROTHERS

ORVILLE and Wilbur Wright did not invent the airplane. Their great contribution to flight was that they were the first to successfully combine the four elements of true aviation—pilot, power, control, and sustained flight. On December 17, 1903, on the sand dunes of Kitty Hawk, North Carolina, Orville Wright (who was pilot that day because he won a coin toss) launched the *Flyer* off a trolley rail into headwinds so strong that his older brother, Wilbur, was able to run alongside it for the duration of the flight, twelve seconds.

◁ Wilbur loses the toss of the coin.

1901, Pablo Picasso's Blue Period begins • 1902, Beatrix Potter's *The Tale of Peter Rabbit* published

1905, Albert Einstein devises the Special Theory of Relativity • 1907, first daily comic strip, "Mutt

THE FIRST HELICOPTER

NEARLY four years after Kitty Hawk, on November 13, 1907, the world's first true helicopter flew free into the air at Lisieux, France. It was a clunky, twin-rotor-bladed, gasoline-powered machine built by a French mechanic named Paul Cornu. Its first flight lasted about twenty seconds and lifted itself and its builder twelve inches off the ground. When the experiment was tried a second time, the machine took off so quickly that it unexpectedly hoisted Cornu's very surprised brother aloft as well.

◁ The Cornu brothers between flights.

and Jeff," appears • 1908, FBI established • 1908, first Model T Ford built • 1910, neon light invented

1911, Roald Amundsen reaches the South Pole •1912, *Titanic* sinks •1914, Charlie Chaplin's first movie •

FIGHTERS

Roland Garros, a Frenchman, was caught in Germany the day World War I broke out. His daring escape led Germany to accuse him of being a spy, an accusation Garros resented. He joined the French air force and flew into battle carrying a grudge and a pistol. He quickly realized that from a bouncing airplane he would not be able to shoot down any "Huns" with a pistol. The most accurate way of firing a gun, he reasoned, was straight ahead. So he and his friend, Raymond Saulnier, developed a rudimentary way of synchronizing a machine gun with the spinning propeller. Armed in this manner on April 1, 1915, Garros, flying a Morane-Saulnier Type L, attacked a German plane, shot it down, and became the world's first true fighter pilot.

◁ Garros in his "Parasol" Morane-Saulnier Type L.

1916, Jeannette Rankin becomes the first U.S. congresswoman • 1917, Russian Revolution begins

1919–1933, alcohol restricted in the U.S. under national Prohibition • 1920, American women gain the

CROSSING THE ATLANTIC

THE Atlantic Ocean remained the great barrier until 1919, when a U.S. Navy pilot, Lt.-Cdr. Albert Cushing Read, and his crew made the first successful crossing. Many followed, flying various routes. But Charles Lindbergh was the first to cross the Atlantic nonstop *and* solo. In order to conserve weight for more fuel, he took neither radio nor parachute. He installed an extra fuel tank in front of the cockpit and had to use a periscope to see forward. His plane, called *The Spirit of St. Louis,* took off from Long Island, New York, on May 20 and landed at Le Bourget airport near Paris on May 21, 1927—thirty-three hours and thirty minutes later. Of the 450 gallons of fuel he began with, only 84 gallons remained.

◁ *The Spirit of St. Louis somewhere over the Atlantic.*

right to vote • 1920, first American radio show airs • 1926, A. A. Milne's *Winnie-the-Pooh* published

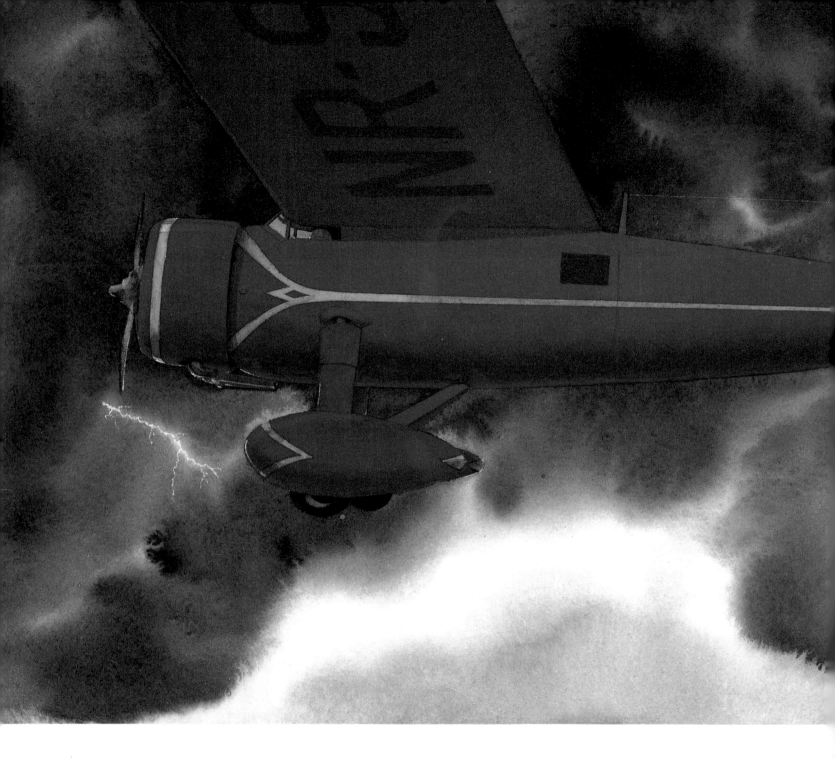

1927, Babe Ruth hits sixty home runs • 1928, first Mickey Mouse film appears • 1929, "talkies" replace

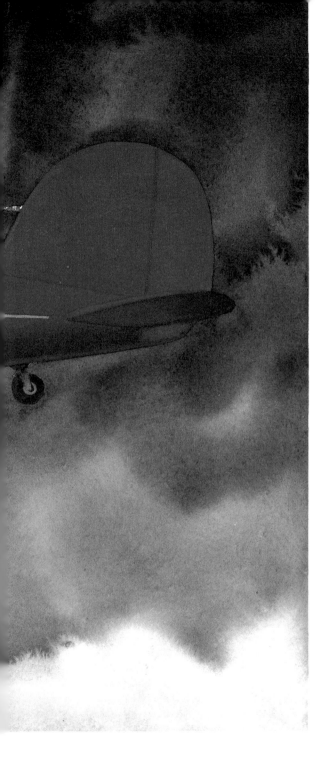

AMELIA EARHART

AMELIA Earhart was the first woman to cross the Atlantic Ocean in an airplane. Her first crossing was in 1928 as a passenger. The second time, May 20, 1932, she flew a bright red Lockheed Vega from Harbour Grace, Newfoundland, to Londonderry, Northern Ireland, solo. Three months later she became the first woman to fly solo across the United States, taking off from Los Angeles, California, and landing in Newark, New Jersey. She was also the first person, man *or* woman, to fly solo across the Pacific Ocean from Honolulu, Hawaii, to Oakland, California. This was on January 12, 1935. But on July 2, 1937, Earhart disappeared during an attempt to circumnavigate the globe.

◁ Earhart's Vega approaching a storm.

1930, planet Pluto discovered • 1930, first supermarket opens • 1930, first commercial freezing o

SPEED

AIR races, a popular event of the 1930s, demanded greater and greater speed, which in turn provided the impetus for technological advances in the structure and design of airplanes. One such airplane was the bizarre little Gee Bee, which made its first appearance at the Thompson Trophy race in 1931. It was designed by the Granville Brothers (hence its name: G-B) in Springfield, Massachusetts, and was little more than an engine with an airframe around it. Nimble, fast, and dangerous, every Gee Bee the Granvilles built crashed at some time or another, many of them fatally. Jimmy Doolittle won the 1932 races in a Gee Bee with a speed of 252.7 mph.

◁ Doolittle wins the Bendix Speed Race.

1932, Franklin D. Roosevelt elected president • 1933, Adolf Hitler becomes chancellor of Germany

WITHOUT A PROPELLER

PROPELLERLESS airplanes remained only an idea until June 11, 1928, when Frederich Stamer flew the first rocket-propelled airplane in the Rhön Mountains in Germany. Then, in the 1930s, Frank Whittle and Hans von Ohain developed the first true air-breathing turbojets—Whittle in England and von Ohain in Germany. They were both successful, but von Ohain's Heinkel He.178 was the first to fly, on August 27, 1939. The Gloster-Whittle E.28/39 Meteor took to the air on May 15, 1941.

◁ The wooden-winged Heinkel He.178.

1936, Spanish Civil War begins • 1936, Jesse Owens wins four gold medals at the Berlin Olympics

TRAVEL BY AIR

IN THE United States civil aviation grew very rapidly between the world wars, more so than anywhere else in the world. In 1933 the Boeing Aircraft Company built the first modern airliner, the Boeing 247. Almost three years later the Douglas Aircraft Company built the first DC-3. One of the most reliable airplanes ever built, it cruised at 180 mph and carried twenty-one passengers. It was so comfortable that, by 1939, the DC-3 carried almost all the air passengers in the world. Because of its enduring dependability and its superior design and construction, many are still in service today.

◁ A DC-3 on a night flight.

1941, first computers built • 1942, Japanese Americans interned in detention camps • 1943, the AI

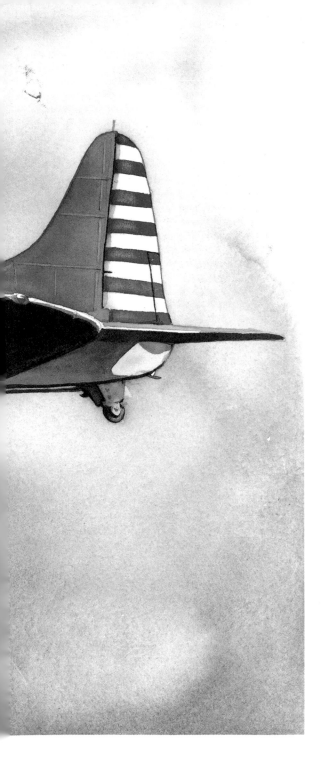

NAVAL AVIATION

NAVAL aviation began in England, the United States, and Japan at the end of World War I. It was in the caldron of World War II, however, that the United States and Japan perfected carrier warfare. The United States' entry into the war was in response to the Japanese carrier-based air strike against its naval base at Pearl Harbor, Hawaii. In 1942 the use of naval air power made the Battle of the Coral Sea the first naval battle in history in which opposing fleets never came within gun range or sight of each other. Few developments in aviation history had such grave and profound ramifications.

◁ A "Slow But Deadly" SBD-3 from the U.S.S. Enterprise.

merican Girls Professional Baseball League begun • 1945, atomic bomb dropped on Hiroshima, Japan

1945, United Nations established •1947, Anne Frank's *The Diary of a Young Girl* published •1948, long

BEYOND THE SOUND BARRIER

ON TUESDAY, October 14, 1947, an orange Bell X-1—nicknamed "Glamorous Glennis" and piloted by Glennis's then-unknown husband, Charles "Chuck" Yeager—was dropped from the belly of a modified Boeing B-29 bomber over the Mojave Desert in Nevada. Burning a mixture of ethyl alcohol and liquid oxygen, the little rocket-powered bullet became the first airplane to burst through the sound barrier.

◁ "Glamorous Glennis" at 43,000 feet.

1950–1953, Korean War • 1954, Supreme Court rules public-school segregation is unconstitutional

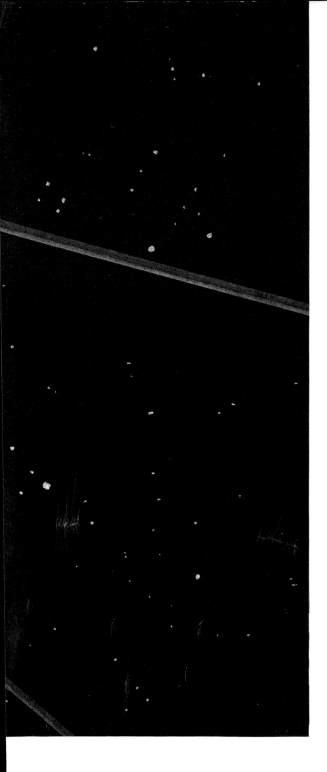

SPUTNIK I

HUMANKIND'S first thrust into space came on October 4, 1957, when a 96-foot-high Soviet military rocket, generating over a million pounds of thrust, inserted a 184-pound artificial satellite into an elliptical orbit around Earth. For three weeks the satellite sent home valuable scientific information. It was called Sputnik, which means "fellow traveler" in Russian. The Earth's first artificial satellite burned up on its reentry into Earth's atmosphere on January 4, 1958.

◁ Sputnik I. A new age begins.

955, Great Britain begins construction of the first nuclear power plant • 1960–73, Vietnam War

1974, President Richard Nixon resigns • 1979–1981, Americans held hostage in Iran • 1980, Joh

GOSSAMER WINGS

ON AUGUST 23, 1977, near Shafter, California, the *Gossamer Condor*, an airplane designed by Paul MacReady that weighed 70 pounds and had a wingspan of 96 feet, took off under human power. It flew for seven and a half minutes, controlled by its pilot, Bryan Allen, a competition bicyclist, who also powered the craft by pedaling a recumbent, bicycle-like apparatus, which in turn drove a propeller.

◁ The *Gossamer Condor* at sunset.

1986, Chernobyl nuclear power plant accident • 1989, Berlin Wall falls • 1991, Persian Gulf War • 1991

NOW AND BEYOND

AMERICA'S first space station, *Skylab*, was placed in Earth orbit on May 14, 1973.

Columbia, the first reusable manned space vehicle, was launched from Pad 39A at Cape Canaveral, Florida, on April 12, 1981, carrying John W. Young as commander and Robert L. Crippin as pilot.

The Soviet Union's first shuttle, *Buran* ("Snowstorm"), was launched on November 15, 1988. The Russian space station *Mir* ("Peace") is currently in orbit.

Since *Columbia*'s maiden flight four other American shuttles joined its ranks—*Discovery*, *Challenger*, *Atlantis*, and *Endeavour*. From such aircraft, and from space stations like the Russian *Mir* and the American *Freedom*, the stage is set for the next adventure in aviation.

◁ The space shuttle *Atlantis*.

.S.S.R. dissolved and Commonwealth of Independent States formed • 1992, Los Angeles race riots

Francesco de Lana-Terzi's flying machine

Joseph Montgolfier

Étienne Montgolfier

HISTORICAL NOTES

The Chinese and the Australian Aborigines were the first to attain flight: the Chinese with kites, the Aborigines with boomerangs. The boomerang, with its cambered (arched) surfaces, is a more sophisticated flying device than the kite, yet it developed in a far less sophisticated society. As early as the sixth century B.C. the Chinese had used kites for various military purposes, such as carrying signals aloft, helping to calculate distances on battlefields, and ultimately to drop bombs on enemies. In the thirteenth century A.D. Marco Polo returned from China (then called Cathay by Europeans) and reported seeing kites carrying men aloft.

In 1250 Roger Bacon, a Franciscan monk from Ilchester, England, wrote a work titled *Secrets of Art and Nature* wherein he suggested the use of mechanical devices and "liquid fire" to navigate the air. Bacon's work preceded that of Leonardo da Vinci by over two hundred years.

It was Leonardo da Vinci, however, who first imagined the true and practical essence of flight for man. Not only was Leonardo one of the great artists of the fifteenth century, he was also an architect, an engineer, and an inventor and scientist whose vision was centuries ahead of his own time. His obsession with flight, and his studies of the anatomy of birds and the physics of their flight, led him to design a birdlike flying machine called an ornithopter, an airscrew helicopter, and a parachute. Though none of his designs were realized in any practical, working models, his ideas were strongly influential on all future pioneers of aviation.

In 1670 a Jesuit priest, Francesco de Lana-Terzi, proposed the first known design for a lighter-than-air machine. It was composed of a ship's hull, a mast, and four copper globes from which all the air would be pumped out. These he thought would yield enough buoyancy to "float" the machine in the air. Of course it never worked, but his heart and mind were in the right place.

THE FIRST ASCENT

On August 8, 1709, a Brazilian priest, Bartolomeu De Gusmão, amazed the court of King John V of Portugal with a working paper model of a hot-air balloon. Seventy-three years later, in France, Joseph Montgolfier developed what he called a "fire balloon." Montgolfier did not recognize that lift came from hot air alone, thinking erroneously that it came from special properties of the gas given off by burning a mixture of straw and wool. Nevertheless, he has traditionally been credited with the invention of lighter-than-air craft. Montgolfier's balloon made its first public flight in Annonay, France, on June 4, 1783, carrying neither passengers nor payload. Then, in September of that same year, Montgolfier and his brother, Étienne, sent up their now-famous duck, sheep, and rooster in an uncontrolled, two-mile flight. All three animals survived, though the rooster suffered a broken wing, having been kicked by the sheep either before or during the flight. We don't know what happened to the duck and the rooster, but the sheep lived out its days pleasantly in the Royal Menagerie of the French King Louis XVI.

The Montgolfiers' experiment with animals proved to them that the air above was breathable, and this set the stage for the first human ascent, on October 15, 1783, when Jean François Pilâtre de Rozier, a twenty-nine-year-old Parisian physicist and chemist, took off in the very same balloon that had carried the animals aloft the month before. The king had suggested that two capital criminals be the crew, but Pilâtre de Rozier objected, saying that this was too great an honor to be given to murderers. He prevailed and became the first man in the western world to fly.

Pilâtre de Rozier's flight was carefully controlled. His balloon was tethered to the ground and rose only to the length of its ropes, an altitude of about 80 feet. After a few more experimental, tethered flights, Pilâtre de Rozier and François Laurent, the Marquis d'Arlandes, cut the tethers and took to the air from the gardens of the Château de la Muette in the Bois de Boulogne. They were airborne about twenty-five minutes, during which time they had an on-board fire and nearly crashed twice. They came to rest about five miles from where they took off. It was November 21, 1783. Benjamin Franklin was among the spectators.

Pilâtre de Rozier also became the first aerial fatality, along with a companion, Pierre-Ange Romain. They died on June 15, 1785, trying to cross the English Channel in a balloon.

THE FIRST FLIGHT

While France can claim the first ascent in a balloon, the first human flight in a heavier-than-air craft took place in Yorkshire, England, in the spring of 1849—at Brompton

Sir George Cayley

Otto Lilienthal

Clement Ader's Éole

Hall, near Scarborough, the home of the baronet Sir George Cayley. After some forty years of experimenting with the designs of scale- and full-sized models, George Cayley's triplane glider became airborne, with a ten-year-old boy strapped into it. Unfortunately, the boy's name and the exact date were not recorded. This first "man-carrying" glide took place at least fifty years after Cayley had first conceived the idea of a fixed-wing aircraft and fifty-four years before the Wright brothers' famous flight at Kitty Hawk.

The contributions George Cayley made to aviation were far more significant than merely floating a small boy off into the air. Cayley, an inventor and theoretician, was the first to establish the mathematical principles of flight—lift, drag, and thrust; he invented the horizontal rudder, which we now call the elevator; he considered the advantages of streamlining forms to reduce drag; he promoted multiple-wing designs; and he envisioned the propeller.

In 1853, again at Brompton Hall, Sir George convinced a doubtful coachman to sail aloft in one of his gliders. The man did as he was asked, and became the second human to fly in a heavier-than-air craft. He apparently landed safely enough, but not without a few bumps and frights. When he had climbed out of the craft and dusted himself off, he said to his employer, "Please, Sir George, I wish to give my notice. I was hired to drive, not to fly!"

OTTO LILIENTHAL

Otto Lilienthal did not invent the airplane, but he was the first man to fly and *control* the flight of a heavier-than-air craft. In 1891—two years after publishing a study on the flight of birds, *Bird Flight as the Basis of Aviation*—he built his first true glider. It was made of bamboo and cane, covered with unbleached cotton muslin. It had a wingspan of about 23 feet, weighed 45 pounds, and bore an astonishing resemblance to a modern hang glider.

Lilienthal, a manufacturer of boilers, pulleys, and sirens, believed that one could learn to fly only by *flying*. And fly he did, more than any man before him had ever done. In addition to using the hills near his home outside Berlin, Lilienthal commandeered a forty-foot-high, cone-shaped mound of rejected bricks from a defunct brick factory in Lichterfeld. He called it his "Flying Hill," and from it he could fly into the wind regardless of the wind's direction. People came from all around, especially on sunny weekends, to watch the redheaded "Birdman" fly, and to perhaps purchase one of his gliders. Lilienthal saw gliding as a sport and built gliders to sell as well as to fly.

Wearing a red sweater, knickers, and high-topped shoes, he made over two thousand flights off "Flying Hill," continually incorporating his experiences into designs for better and stronger gliders and longer flights. He was confident that he could achieve powered flight if and when a suitable power plant was invented.

Since his flights were the first to be photographed, Lilienthal's influence was felt throughout the aviation community, and nowhere more profoundly than in Dayton, Ohio, in the bicycle shop of Orville and Wilbur Wright.

Otto Lilienthal died of a broken back resulting from the crash of one of his biplane gliders in 1896. Had he survived the crash, Lilienthal might very well have been the first man to achieve true powered flight. His last words were "Sacrifices must be made."

THE WRIGHT BROTHERS

What is unique about the Wright brothers' famous flight at Kitty Hawk, North Carolina, on December 17, 1903, and what makes it the most important moment in the history of aviation, is that for the first time the four elements of true aviation were combined—pilot, power, control, and sustained flight. Orville Wright controlled the *Flyer* with forward elevators, aft rudders, and warping (bending) of the flexible wing surfaces. Power was supplied by a twelve-horsepower gasoline engine that the Wrights and their mechanic, Charles Taylor, had built themselves. Long bicycle chains connected the engine to two propellers, which pushed the airplane through air for twelve seconds and a distance of 120 feet.

The first powered aircraft became airborne on October 9, 1890, in Armainvilliers near Gretz, France; it was a steam-driven machine, called the *Éole,* and was manned by its designer, Clement Ader. The flight was 55 yards by Ader's account, but he could not maneuver the craft. He again "almost flew" in 1891, but the *Éole* hit a wagon and crashed.

An American, Samuel Pierpont Langley, designed and flew a small, unpiloted steam-powered aircraft, his *Aerodrome #5*, several times on May 6, 1896. It had two tandem wings about 13 feet in span, and was about 16 feet long. It was powered by a two-cylinder steam engine and flew with remarkable stability, one time covering over 3,000 feet. In 1903 Langley installed a five-cylinder, 52-horsepower engine into a full-scale version of the 1896 model, called the *Aerodrome.* With the engine's designer, Charles Manley, as pilot, he launched the craft from a catapult on the Potomac River at Widewater. While it is to-

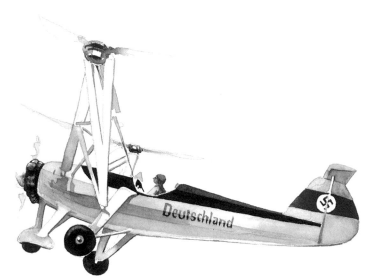

The Focke-Achgelis Fa 61

Anthony Fokker

Roland Garros

day recognized as the first aircraft that was capable of flight, it did not fly, and it prompted an editor of *The New York Times* to comment that it was a fiasco, and that, perhaps, if we combined the "continuous efforts of mathematicians and mechanicians" and eliminated the "existing relation between weight and strength in inorganic materials," a true flying machine might be "evolved" in "from one to ten million years." Just two months later, the Wright brothers succeeded at Kitty Hawk.

THE FIRST HELICOPTER

Of the Wright brothers' success, Thomas Edison said that flight would never be practical until the aircraft could land and take off *vertically*.

The idea of vertical flight is at least 700 years old, dating to the twelfth-century Chinese invention of the "flying top." It was a child's toy made up of a dowel with three propellerlike wings affixed to one end. Like a top, it was whirled into flight by a quick pull of a cord. In the fifteenth century, Leonardo da Vinci made a drawing of an "airscrew," a flying machine that he imagined as literally "screwing" its way through the air powered by four men pushing turn bars. It was in fact Leonardo who invented the word "helicopter" by combining the two Greek words *helix* (spiral) and *pteron* (wing).

It is said that a Russian, Mikhail Lomonosov, may have flown a clockwork model helicopter in 1754. Even Sir George Cayley played with the idea around 1843. It was not until 1907, however, that a true helicopter that could actually fly was designed and built. It was built by Louis and Jacques Breguet and Charles Richet. It was designed to lift only its own weight off the ground, which it did—all of two feet. In additional tests the Breguet-Richet "gyroplane" gained an altitude of five feet, but the machine never flew free of the control of its ground crew. That same year saw the experiments of Paul Cornu succeed, his machine ultimately lifting itself, Cornu, and Cornu's brother five feet off the ground. The total weight was 720 pounds.

While Cornu's primitive helicopter was the first to rise, another thirty years would pass before Heinrich Focke would design the world's first practical helicopter, the Focke-Achgelis Fa 61. It ascended to 7,700 feet, flew forward at 75 mph and backward at 20 mph, and covered 140 miles in a straight line. Developed in secrecy, its first public demonstration was in Berlin in 1938. The pilot was a woman, Hanna Reitsch.

FIGHTERS

The Wright brothers thought, when they built and flew their flying machine, that they were introducing into the world an invention that would make future wars impossible. Unfortunately, such was not the case.

As terrible a thing as World War I was, it gave enormous momentum, energy, and technical and financial resources to the fledgling aviation industry. At the beginning of the war in 1914, England and France together had only two hundred or so aircraft on the western front. At the close of the war in 1918, England alone had over twenty-two thousand. At the beginning of the war civilian pilots were conscripted for service (drafted) because the military had yet to be convinced that aircraft could be effective for anything other than observation and reconnaissance. It didn't take long for resourceful pilots to begin throwing darts, firing pistols, dropping hand grenades, and taking potshots at each other with rifles and machine guns. But holding a shoulder weapon while flying a plane with the knees proved to be risky business: Since pilots did not use seat belts at that time, a few unfortunate warriors fell out of their planes.

It is interesting to note that even though the U.S. Army Air Service required all personnel flying aircraft to wear parachutes in 1919, for various reasons, including the lack of suitable parachutes, it was not until 1920 that the habit of wearing them was firmly established for all army fliers. The first emergency use of a parachute was by Lt. Harold Harris on October 20, 1922. On March 21, 1924, the U.S. Navy directed that "parachutes be used by all personnel on all flights."

Eventually machine guns were installed on the aircraft, but when they were mounted in the only really effective position, directly in front of the pilot's windshield, they had an unfortunate tendency to shoot off the propeller blades. French pilots prevented this with modest success by fitting the aft sides of their propellers with steel plates to deflect the bullets (about one in ten bullets struck the propeller).

By 1915, Anthony Fokker, inspired by the synchronizing device his assistants found on Roland Garros's downed Morane-Saulnier L, perfected the idea of synchronizing the engine speed, the propeller, and the machine gun, so that the bullets fired through the propeller's arc without hitting the blades no matter how many revolutions per minute the aircraft's engine was doing. German air superiority resulted from Fokker's device, a superiority that became known to British, French, and American pilots as the "Fokker scourge."

A. C. "Putty" Read

Charles Lindbergh

The Curtiss NC-4

CROSSING THE ATLANTIC

As aircraft became more sophisticated and aviators more skilled and daring, barriers fell: speed and altitude first, then endurance and geography. Louis Blériot flew across the English Channel in 1909, George Chavez crossed the Alps in 1910, and Roland Garros crossed the Mediterranean in 1913.

The headline *"L'Atlantique est traversé"* ("The Atlantic Is Crossed") appeared on the front page of a Parisian newspaper on May 9, 1927. It proudly announced still yet another French milestone in aviation: the first nonstop east-to-west transatlantic flight, by *L'Oiseau Blanc,* piloted by François Coli and Charles Nungesser. Unfortunately, the story was not true. In fact, *L'Oiseau Blanc* had vanished without a trace. Nevertheless, the flight of that "White Bird" was the first of several attempts in the spring and summer of 1927 to cross the Atlantic Ocean by air.

The Atlantic was first crossed in May of 1919. A U.S. Navy pilot, Albert Cushing "Putty" Read, captained a Curtiss NC-4 flying boat and its crew of six across the ocean, taking off from Rockaway Beach, Long Island, stopping in Newfoundland and the Azores, and terminating on the Tagus River in Lisbon, Portugal, nineteen days later. In June of the same year two British pilots, John Alcock and Arthur Whitten-Brown, set off from St. John's, Newfoundland, and flew nonstop 1,900 miles to Clifden, Ireland. In 1924 a Portuguese team, Sacadura Cabral and Cago Coutinho, crossed the South Atlantic from Lisbon to Rio de Janeiro via the Canaries and the Cape Verde Islands. That crossing took seventy-nine days due to mechanical problems and bad weather.

But no one had yet crossed the Atlantic nonstop *and* alone. That distinction was captured, along with a $25,000 prize, by the American pilot Charles Lindbergh. His Ryan monoplane was named *The Spirit of St. Louis* because it was bought for him by a group of businessmen from the city of St. Louis, Missouri. Two thousand dollars of the total $15,000 cost of the Ryan was Lindbergh's own money.

Scarcely three weeks later, June 4–6, Clarence Chamberlain and the first transatlantic passenger, Charles Levine, flew from New York to Eisleben, Germany.

And then, three weeks after that, a crew led by Cdr. Richard E. Byrd, one of the first men to cross the North Pole, took off from New York to Cherbourg, France. Although they nearly reached landfall, bad weather and empty fuel tanks forced them to put down in the sea near Calvados, France. All together, there were four successful crossings and five failed attempts to cross the Atlantic in 1927.

AMELIA EARHART

The desire to fly is not the dream of men alone. Women, too, have dreamed the dream of Leonardo and have been part of flying from the very beginning. The first woman aeronaut was Jeanne-Genevieve Garnerin, a balloonist who also happened to be the first woman parachutist. Garnerin was killed in 1819 falling from her balloon, which had caught fire. Eugenie and Fanny Godard were part of a famous ballooning family in the 1830s. In a 1909 demonstration, Mrs. Cromwell Dixon pedaled a dirigible-like airship, *Dixon's-Air-Ship*, which was built by her thirteen-year-old son, Cromwell, Jr., who called it an "air bicycle." Cromwell Dixon, Jr., himself was also one of the earliest American aeronauts.

The first woman to fly in a heavier-than-air machine was the French sculptor Thérèse Peltier, who took to the air in Milan, Italy, on July 8, 1908, with the sculptor-turned-aviator Léon Delegrange. Later, Peltier became the first woman to fly solo. She never formally qualified as a pilot, however. The distinction of being the first qualified woman pilot went to Raymonde de Laroach, who got her pilot's license on March 8, 1910.

In 1928 Lady Mary Heath was the first woman to fly from Cape Town, South Africa, to London, England. Lady Heath shunned the male dress adopted by most women pilots and flew over the African jungles in a dress, fur coat, and high-heeled shoes. Her aircraft was painted turquoise blue to match her favorite ring. In 1932 the Frenchwoman Maryse Bastié flew alone longer than any man had yet done—thirty-eight hours. And five years to the day after Charles Lindbergh flew solo across the Atlantic, Amelia Earhart did the same thing in half the time.

SPEED

Sixteen years after Kitty Hawk airplanes flying at speeds in excess of 100 mph were commonplace. Once a new speed record was established, it was immediately challenged, often at air races and exhibitions. Speed and endurance records fell regularly as more powerful engines were employed and better designs developed. For example, in 1913 the Michelin Cup race required pilots to fly specific distances while maintaining an average speed of 31 mph; then in that same year the Gordon Bennett Trophy was won by Jules Vedrines with a speed of over 100

Thérèse Peltier

Amelia Earhart

The Opel rocket-powered airplane

The Boeing 247

mph. Seven years later, on November 26, 1920, Sadi Lecointe, flying a 300-horsepower Nieuport-Hispano at Étampes, France, became the first human to exceed 200 mph. On October 18, 1922, Billy Mitchell set a new world record in the Pulitzer race at 222 mph. Jimmy Doolittle set the world record for seaplanes in 1925 with a speed of 233 mph.

Speeds like this were extremely stressful on airplanes—shattering propellers, peeling off surfaces, and ripping apart fuselages. Solving these problems made fundamental design changes evolve that pointed the way to the future: strutless monoplanes, streamlined forms, lighter construction, variable wing curvature, retractable landing gear, and adjustable flaps.

These new designs served speed and maneuverability, premiums for military purposes. And since speed reduces time and navigational problems, commercial passenger service benefited as well.

Many of the racing airplanes and pilots had significant military influence. The renowned Spitfire, for instance, was developed by the designers of the Supermarine S-5 and S-6 seaplanes, which won the Schneider Trophy more than once. A Messerschmitt Bf 109 took the world speed record to 379 mph in 1938. During World War II Jimmy Doolittle led the first air strike against the Japanese mainland flying a B-25 Mitchell medium bomber named after Billy Mitchell.

WITHOUT A PROPELLER

The speed of a propeller-driven airplane is limited, because the speed of the tip of a spinning propeller must always be greater than the speed of the airplane itself.

Thus, when an airplane is flying at 450 mph, the tip speed of the propeller becomes supersonic, and this results in a lessening of the rearward thrust of the propeller. It was from this phenomenon and from the drive for greater speed that the turbojet engine was developed.

The principle was not new: Isaac Newton had observed that for every action there is an equal and opposite reaction—the basic idea of jet propulsion. The Chinese invented the rocket about A.D. 1100. The Montgolfier brothers envisioned jet propulsion for their balloons in 1763. And Charles de Louvrié designed a true jet-propelled aircraft in 1865, though he never tried to build it.

Even though Frederich Stamer made the first rocket-propelled flight in 1928, followed by Fritz von Opel in 1929, true air-breathing jet propulsion was not developed for another year, until, in England, a twenty-three-year-old Royal Air Force officer named Frank Whittle filed for a patent on a design for a turbojet engine. Whittle tested his turbojet successfully in 1937 and attracted his government's interest and money. In 1941 his engine powered an airplane in flight, the Gloster-Whittle E.28/39 Meteor.

Meanwhile, in Germany in 1935, a young German physicist, Hans von Ohain, applied for a patent for a similar engine. His turbojet was developed by the Heinkel company and was put into the experimental Heinkel He.178 plane, which took its maiden flight on August 27, 1939, thus becoming the first true jet-propelled airplane.

TRAVEL BY AIR

Despite the many advances in aviation brought about by World War I—better design of airplanes and their power plants, endurance potential, numbers of manufacturing plants, numbers of trained aviators, distances traveled, and obstacles overcome—by the end of the war in 1918, there was not a single aircraft designed to carry passengers.

After the war a few military airplanes were converted to civil use, particularly the large bombers like the Farman F-60 Goliath, which made the first international passenger flight, from Paris to London on February 5, 1919, carrying eleven passengers. (It should be noted that a domestic passenger flight had been made three days earlier by a company called Deutche Luftreederei from Berlin to Leipzig and Weimar.)

Because of the huge geographic scale and tremendous industrial capacity of the United States after the war, civil aviation developed very rapidly, beginning with cargo transport and mail. In fact, Charles Lindbergh logged many hours flying mail between Chicago and St. Louis two years before he crossed the Atlantic, an idea that had occurred to him on one of his runs.

The first modern airliner, the Boeing 247, took its maiden flight on February 8, 1933. It could carry ten passengers and flew at 150 mph. Unlike its predecessors, the awkward Ford Tri-Motor and the Boeing Model 80 (both of which flew scheduled airline routes), the Boeing 247 had low wings, twin engines, and the clean lines that set the standard for airliner design for a generation to come.

But of all the passenger airplanes built at that time, none surpassed the Douglas Aircraft Company's DC-3. Its first flight was on December 17, 1935. Also designated as the C-47 (C for Cargo), it was variously called the Dakota, the Skytrain, and, affectionately, the Gooney Bird, and saw service as a highly successful military transport in World War II. By the time the last DC-3 rolled off the as-

Isoroku Yamamoto

Chuck Yeager

The Mitsubishi A6M Zero

sembly line in 1945, 13,000 had been built. Many of these venerable old airplanes are still in active service today.

The designs of the 247 and the DC-3 were so advanced that a traveler is hard put not to notice the echoes of their designs in the noses of all the modern airliners, such as the DC-10 and the 727.

NAVAL AVIATION

The failure of the Disarmament Conference in October 1933 caused an "air arms race" to break out in Europe. By 1936 the modern warplane had been born. Many of the finest combat airplanes of World War II had been prototyped by 1936: the British Hurricane and Supermarine Spitfire; the German Messerschmidt Bf 109 and the Junkers Ju 87 Stuka; the Boeing B-17 Flying Fortress; the Japanese Nakajima Ki-27.

It was in fact one of these airplanes—a Junkers Stuka—that lit the fires of World War II when it dive-bombed the railway bridge at Tczew, Poland, on September 1, 1939. And from that day until the last day of the war, when the Japanese surrendered on September 2, 1945, aviation proved itself to be an indisputable battle force.

By the time World War II began, engineers, designers, and strategists had developed more powerful engines, streamlined designs, all-metal construction, in-flight refueling, pressurized cabins, high-altitude performance, retractable landing gear, highly efficient weapons systems, parachuting, supercharged engines, radar, and long-range bombers with fighter escorts. They had all but abandoned the biplane and had developed operational jet-propelled airplanes, though only the German turbojets saw action.

No development, however, was as significant as that of aircraft-carrier warfare. The idea was first conceived by a young Japanese naval officer, Isoroku Yamamoto, during the Russo-Japanese war in 1904–5. Later, as an admiral in the Japanese navy, Yamamoto became the architect of the air strike against Pearl Harbor.

The first attack from an aircraft carrier's flight deck was launched by the British on July 19, 1918, when seven Sopwith Camels from the converted cruiser *Furious* successfully bombed a Zeppelin base.

The first Japanese vessel dedicated to carrying airplanes was the *Hosho*, which was laid down on December 19, 1919, launched on November 13, 1921, and completed in December of 1922.

The first ship actually designed as a carrier, however, was the British *Hermes*, which was laid down in 1918, launched on September 11, 1919, and completed in July of 1923. The British had four carriers in service at that time, compared to one each for America and Japan. Even though the Royal Navy had made the faster start, it was surpassed by the Pacific powers in 1941.

Since offensive strikes against warships could be achieved only by bomb, or torpedoes, new breeds of fighters and divebombers were developed along with the torpedo bomber: the Mitsubishi A6M Zero, the Aichi D3A1 Val, the Nakajima B5N Kate, the Curtiss SB2C Helldiver, the Grumman F4F Wildcat, the Douglas SBD Dauntless, the Vought F4U Corsair.

The first bombing strikes against the Japanese mainland by U.S. airplanes were staged off an aircraft carrier. On April 18, 1942, Lt. General Jimmy Doolittle led a squadron of sixteen B-25 medium bombers off the U.S.S. *Hornet*, flying 645 miles to bomb Tokyo, Nagoya, Osaka, and Kobe. After striking their targets, the B-25s continued on to China, where the crews bailed out when the airplanes ran out of fuel. One of the B-25s was diverted to Siberia and was the only one of the sixteen to land safely.

BEYOND THE SOUND BARRIER

During World War II, pilots often encountered violent jouncing and jolting of their airplanes when, in high-speed dives, they approached the speed of sound (about 760 mph at sea level). This shaking and buffeting often threw airplanes out of control and ripped off wings.

Nevertheless, the desire for faster, high-performance military airplanes demanded that designers and engineers develop machines that could penetrate this so-called "sound barrier."

The sound barrier occurs because as an airplane flies, it displaces air; the air forms disturbances called pressure waves, which, like ripples in water, move away from the plane in all directions. At the speed of sound the airplane and pressure waves are moving at the same velocity. When the airplane exceeds the speed of its own pressure waves, it is said to "break the sound barrier."

It is virtually impossible for a propeller-driven airplane to break the sound barrier, and thus it was thought for a long time that the barrier was simply impenetrable. Many airplanes and pilots were lost trying to prove that it wasn't before Chuck Yeager's orange Bell X-1 pierced the invisible wall 43,000 feet above the Mojave Desert.

Since bullets were known to be supersonic, it was logical for the design and shape of the X-1 to result from a study of .50-caliber bullets. It had stubby wings that could withstand eighteen times the force of gravity and

The V-2 rocket

Konstantin Tsiolkovsky

Laika

was powered by four rocket motors, each producing 1,500 pounds of thrust. Two tons of fuel were consumed per minute at full throttle, a condition that could be tolerated for only two and a half minutes.

By 1949 the Bell X-1 had attained a speed of 967 mph and an altitude of over 70,000 feet. Yeager pushed a later model of the Bell X-1, the Bell X-1A, to a speed of 1,650 mph. The little rocketship retired in 1950, but not before it and its intrepid pilots had set into motion the inspiration and the machinery that would ultimately land Neil Armstrong and Edwin Aldrin on the moon.

SPUTNIK I

One of the ironies of war is that it often produces astonishing technologies, such as plastic surgery and advanced aviation, which are ultimately beneficial rather than destructive to humankind.

Rocketry is such a technology. Although the history of rockets dates back some eleven hundred years to Chinese "fire arrows," it was Germany that developed the first tactical rocket weapon, the V-2 (the V stood for *Vergeltung*, meaning retaliation or reprisal in German), which terrorized London during World War II from September 8, 1944, to March 27, 1945. After the war German rocket scientists dispersed, some to the United States, some to what was then called the Soviet Union. With their help the Soviets and Americans alike modified V-2s not only into more sophisticated rockets, but also into weapons of destruction—ballistic missiles. Ultimately, however, these ballistic missiles were themselves adapted to carry peaceful and scientific payloads into space.

The first such payload was the 184-pound artificial satellite called Sputnik I. A month later, in an event reminiscent of the Montgolfiers' sending the duck, rooster, and sheep aloft, another satellite, Sputnik II (sometimes referred to jokingly as "Muttnik"), blasted into space carrying a perk-eared, 40-pound dog name Laika. Laika died when his ten-day supply of oxygen ran out.

All the while, pilots continued to fly more-or-less conventional aircraft to the outer edges of the atmosphere, most notably in the rocket-powered X-15, which in 1967 flew at 4,534 mph and achieved an altitude of 354,200 feet (67 miles).

Then on July 21, 1969, after scores of successful experiments, including the Soviets' putting the first man in orbit and landing an unmanned craft on the moon, two Americans, Neil Armstrong (who carried with him a piece of the original fabric from the Wright *Flyer*) and Edwin Aldrin, stepped out of their Apollo II lunar module and imbedded in the dusty, still surface of the moon the first footprints of humankind.

GOSSAMER WINGS

In the ninety-year period of their existence, aircraft have developed to such a level of sophistication and complexity that many modern aircraft are impossible for a human to fly without the aid of computerized backup systems.

To some it seemed that the purity of flight had become sullied by speed and power and altitude, and so the dream and challenge of elementary, human-powered flight arose again in the 1970s in Japan, France, England, and America with aircraft named *Puffin*, and *Linnett*, and *Liverpuffin*, and *Toucan*, and *Hurel Aviette*, and *Stork*. They all took advantage of modern engineering and strong, light-weight materials, some of which were by-products of the aerospace industry.

The *Puffin* was the first human-powered craft. It was built by Hawker-Siddeley in England, constructed of aluminum, balsa wood, and sheet plastic, and used a bicycle-like apparatus to turn a propeller for propulsion. It flew over 600 feet before crashing. A second *Puffin*, *Puffin II*, also crashed, and Hawker-Siddeley abandoned the project.

On August 23, 1977, Paul MacReady's *Gossamer Condor* achieved an unassisted takeoff and maintained a sustained, controlled flight by the power of the human body alone. On June 12, 1979, Bryan Allen flew a cousin of the *Gossamer Condor*, the *Gossamer Albatross*, across the English Channel. The duration of that flight was two hours and forty-nine minutes. On July 7, 1981, Steve Ptacek, flying another Gossamer cousin, the *Solar Challenger*, crossed the English Channel in five and a half hours—powered by the sun. Unlike the wax-and-feather wings of Icarus, these wings didn't melt.

NOW AND BEYOND

In 1891 a German, Hermann Ganswindt, designed a spaceship. In 1900 Roman Baron von Gostkowski published a scientific treatise on the possibility of space travel. In 1903, the year of Kitty Hawk, Konstantin Eduardovich Tsiolkovsky, a deaf Russian schoolteacher, published theoretical studies on rocket fuels and motors that laid the foundations of modern astronautics. Tsiolkovsky also envisioned satellites and solar energy and, in a more poetic vein, the socialization of the solar system, the use of plants to provide food and fresh oxygen on long space

Robert Goddard

Hermann Oberth

The U.S.S. Enterprise

voyages, and centrifugal showers for bathing in weightless conditions. He fictionalized his theories in a novel called *Outside the Earth.*

In 1920 Robert Hutchings Goddard was labeled the "Moon-Rocket Man" because he had proposed the possibility of a flight to the moon in a 1919 pamphlet, "A Method of Reaching Extreme Altitudes." *The New York Times* accused him of having no more knowledge than that "daily ladled out in high schools." Six years later, on March 16, 1926, Goddard launched the world's first liquid-fuel rocket on his aunt Effie's farm in Auburn, Massachusetts.

In 1923 a German schoolteacher, Hermann Oberth, published *The Rocket into Interplanetary Space.* In it he arrived at the same conclusions as Tsiolkovsky and Goddard, but went beyond them with his vision of a large, permanent, inhabited satellite space station.

In less than a hundred years their visions have materialized—we have walked on the moon, landed a spacecraft on Mars, and mapped large sectors of Venus. Satellites connect us by telephone and television, bringing us each other's voices, world events, and tomorrow's weather. Plans are underway for an exploratory mission to Neptune and Pluto. And even as we read, *Pioneer* probes are coursing deep into the cosmos bearing images of us *Homo sapiens* and a map of where we live.

The space station *Mir,* put into orbit by the Soviet Union, has been in orbit around Earth for several years, and the United States space station *Freedom* is now poised for completion—if it survives the economics of its time. What a delicious irony it will be if the now-tamed rivalry between two former adversaries (which gave such an enormous boost to the "space race" of the 1960s) should provide the impetus, through cooperation, for an internationally crewed space station.

Current trends in the space-faring world are leaning more and more toward the international. In 1991 students from twenty-six countries worked together at the International Space University to formulate a feasible plan for a human mission to Mars by the year 2017. NASA's Space Mission 42 shuttle project features an International Microgravity Laboratory. And Russia has proposed working closely with the United States in developing nuclear-propelled rockets. If these things happen, it is likely that space-faring crews of the future will bear an uncanny resemblance to the fictional crew of the starship *Enterprise*.

And if this were to be the case, it would not be the first time science fiction has turned to science fact. History has proven that science fiction has had and continues to have a very real and influential role in space exploration. The works of Johannes Kepler, Savinien de Cyrano de Bergerac, Jules Verne, Edward Everett Hale, and H. G. Wells were influential with the early pioneers of astronautics. These works were products of fertile, poetic imaginations, and it must be remembered that imagination is the great seedbed of art, literature, poetry, *and* science. The great Polish-American scientist-philosopher Jacob Bronowski predicted that the greatest artists of the twentieth century will be its scientists. So to the question "Where next?" comes the answer: "One can only imagine."

Remember *The New York Times* reporter saying in 1903 that if certain physical laws were repealed, mathematicians and mechanics might be able to build a flying machine "in from one to ten million years"? This was the comment of an informed but unimaginative person. But no matter. Even if the journalist had been imaginative and poetic and prophetic, he could not have foreseen the profound and awesome developments that the next decade, much less the next hundred years, would hold in store.

So here we stand on the threshold of the twenty-first century. The hundred years of aviation history since Lilienthal are behind us, and *we* try to conjure the future. Our imaginations and powers of prophecy, like the *Times* journalist's, are limited. How can we help but be moved and awed by the proposition that such astonishing developments and inventions may yet come to pass again and that our poets' visions will continue to materialize? To the citizens of Earth in A.D. 2093 the space shuttle *Atlantis* may seem as quaint and curious as Langley's *Aerodrome* does to us today. Who knows but that in the next hundred years aircraft and spacecraft themselves will become a "machine barrier" that will have to be broken, and poets and mathematicians and mechanics will break it and fly neither by Newtonian principles nor on air, but by principles or on elements as yet unknown—in light and time.

BIBLIOGRAPHY

Bowers, Peter M. *The DC-3: 50 Years of Legendary Flight.* Blue Ridge Summit, PA: Tab, 1986.

Boyne, Walter J. *The Smithsonian Book of Flight for Young People.* New York: Macmillan/Aladdin Books, 1988.

Bryan, C. D. *The National Air and Space Museum* (2nd, rev. ed). New York: Abrams, 1988.

Campbell, Christy. *Air War Pacific: The Fight for Supremacy in the Far East: 1937 to 1945.* New York: Crescent, 1990.

Canby, Courtlandt. *A History of Flight.* New York: Hawthorn, 1963.

Clark, Arthur C. *Man and Space.* New York: Time-Life Books, 1964.

Cohen, Stan B. *Destination Tokyo: A Pictorial History of Doolittle's Tokyo Raid.* Missoula, MT: Pictorial Histories, 1983.

Collier's Encyclopedia with Bibliography and Index. New York: Macmillan, 1986, 1992.

Encyclopædia Britannica. Chicago: Encyclopædia Britannica, 1973.

———. *The New Encyclopædia Britannica,* 15th edition. Chicago: Encyclopædia Britannica, 1990.

———. *1990 Britannica Book of the Year.* Chicago: Encyclopædia Britannica, 1990.

———. *1991 Britannica Book of the Year.* Chicago: Encyclopædia Britannica, 1991.

———. *1992 Britannica Book of the Year.* Chicago: Encyclopædia Britannica, 1992.

Freedman, Russell. *The Wright Brothers: How They Invented the Airplane.* New York: Holiday, 1991.

Garber, Paul E. *The National Aeronautics Collection.* Washington, DC: Smithsonian Institution Press, 1956.

Gibbs-Smith, Charles H. *Flight Through the Ages.* New York: Crowell, 1974.

———. *The Invention of the Aeroplane (1799–1909).* London: Faber and Faber, 1966.

Gillispie, Charles. *The Montgolfier Brothers and the Invention of Aviation 1783–1784.* Princeton, NJ: Princeton University Press, 1983.

Golley, John, and William Gunston. *Whittle: The True Story.* Washington, DC: Smithsonian Institution Press, 1987.

Grun, Bernard. *The Timetables of History.* New York: Simon & Schuster, 1975.

Hallion, Richard P. *Supersonic Flight.* New York: Macmillan, 1972.

Jackson, Donald Dale. *The Aeronauts.* Alexandria, VA: Time-Life Books, 1980.

Kennett, Lee. *The First Air War: Nineteen Fourteen to Nineteen Eighteen.* New York: The Free Press/Macmillan, 1990.

Kunhardt, Philip B., Jr., ed. *Life: World War II.* Boston: Little, Brown, 1990.

Lomax, Judy. *Hanna Reitsch: Flying for the Fatherland.* London: J. Murray, 1990.

Long, Michael. *The Flight of the Gossamer Condor.* Washington, DC: National Geographic Magazine, January 1978.

Mackworth-Praed, Ben. *Aviation: The Pioneer Years.* London: Studio Editions, 1990.

Meyer, Robert B., Jr. *Langley's Model Aero Engine of 1903.* Washington, DC: Aeroplanes and Engines Publishers, 1976.

Miller, Jay. *The X-Planes: X-1 to X-29.* New York: Crown, 1988.

Mondey, David, ed. *An Illustrated History of Aircraft.* London: Quarto, 1980.

———. *The Complete Illustrated Encyclopedia of the World's Aircraft.* Secaucus, NJ: Chartwell Books, 1978.

Munson, Kenneth. *Warplanes of Yesteryear.* New York: Arco, 1966.

Norgaard, Eric. *The Book of Balloons.* New York: Crown, 1970.

Park, Edwards. *Fighters: The World's Great Aces and Their Planes.* Charlottesville, VA: Thomasson-Grant, 1990.

Pendray, G. Edward. *The Coming Age of Rocket Power.* New York: Harper, 1945.

Polmar, Norman. *Aircraft Carriers.* Garden City, NY: Doubleday, 1969.

Rolt, L.T.C. *The Aeronauts.* New York: Walker, 1966.

Rosenberry, C. R. *The Challenging Skies: The Colorful Story of Aviation's Most Exciting Years, 1919–1939.* Ed. by James Gilbert. Philadelphia: Ayer, 1966.

Schwipps, Werner. *Lilienthal.* Berlin: Arani Verlag, 1979.

Stever, H. Guyford, and James J. Haggerty. *Flight.* New York: Time-Life Books, 1973.

Tames, Richard. *Amelia Earhart.* New York: F. Watts, 1990.

Taylor, John W. R., ed. *Combat Aircraft of the World from 1909 to the Present.* New York: Putnam, 1969.

Taylor, Michael J. H. *History of Flight.* New York: Crescent, 1990.

Trager, James, ed. *The People's Chronology: A Year-by-Year Record of Human Events from Prehistory to the Present.* New York: Holt, 1979.

Wagner, Ray. *American Combat Planes.* Garden City, NY: Doubleday, 1982.

Yenne, Bill. *The Encyclopedia of U.S. Spacecraft.* Greenwich, CT: Brompton, 1985.